BOOK REVIEW

*. . . 26 new ways to conceal messages with simple,
straightforward directions, examples, and exercises . . .
A fresh treatment of a popular subject.*

from THE BOOKLIST

Weekly Reader Books presents

Code Busters!

BURTON ALBERT, Jr.

Illustrated by Jerry Warshaw

Albert Whitman & Company, Niles, Illinois

HEATHER and KELLEY

This book is a presentation of Weekly Reader Books.
Weekly Reader Books offers book clubs for children
from preschool through high school.

For Further information write to:
Weekly Reader Books
4343 Equity Drive
Columbus, Ohio 43228

Library of Congress Cataloging in Publication Data

Albert, Burton, Jr.
   Code busters!

   Summary: Presents an illustrated explanation of
twenty-five codes that can be used to send secret
messages.
   1. Ciphers—Juvenile literature. [1. Ciphers]
I. Warshaw, Jerry, ill. II. Title.
Z103.3.A52   1985   001.54'36   84-29935
ISBN 0-8075-1235-4

The text of this book is set in twelve-point Helvetica

Shhh! Let's keep it a secret. **CODE BUSTERS!** is here! Whether you're new to the sleuthing game or were one of the spies who loved cracking **CODES FOR KIDS** and **MORE CODES FOR KIDS,** here are wit twisters to ponder over and puzzle out.

Among other things, the codes are disguised by dots and boxes, skyscrapers of color, upper-case letters and lower, phone numbers, musical flags, video screens, card decks, plip-plops, turtles, butterflies, and black-eyed Susans.

Riddles supply laughs—and groans—along the way. And, in case a piece of bafflegab should stump a sleepy sleuth, you can flip to all the decoded messages in the Answer File on page 30.

GUARANTEE: Make sure, of course, no one can follow your footsteps. Take the Code-Cracker's Pledge: do not leave any marks, scribbles, or even the faint hint of any message buried in this book. That way you'll keep sly spies off your trail and, at the same time, guarantee yourself a heap of fun. Enjoy!

BREAKER MAKERS

Buff up your spyglass. Make it sparkle clean and bright. Then snoop your way through each word group below. Scout out the letters that have broken parts or fail to connect at all points. For each sentence, write down the broken letters in the order they come. Then draw lines between certain letters to separate the coded words.

Pay no attention to the unbroken letters. They are misleads. A **mislead** is a letter or word or other mark that keeps a . . .

MESSAGE | HIDDEN.

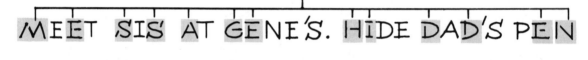

TRY THE KEY: CRACK THE CODES

1 PUSH ON THE DIME.

2 ROSE IS UNDER OUR SPELL.

3 BURR, FIND A RED SKI PULLOVER.

4 JO WILL LOSE VERA'S SALAD.

5 I SENT MY TWO SISTERS WITH A MAP.

Did you crack 'em all? Check. Turn to the Answer File on page 30.

BEGINNER'S SCRAWL

Trick the eye of an eagle beagle. Make a coded message look like the scrawls of a first-grader.

Print your message **backward** —all in lower case, or small, letters:

e o h s

Then plot a trail of misleads. Insert them in upper-case, or capital, letters.

Every once in a while, print a letter backward to befuddle nosy Fidos:

LeoN ChARLEs

LOWER-CASE LETTERS

a b c d e f g h i
j k l m n o p q
r s t u v w x y z

UPPER-CASE LETTERS

A B C D E F G H I
J K L M N O P Q
R S T U V W X Y Z

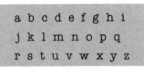

TRY THE KEY: CRACK THE CODES

1 SpuNbEE'S milKcASE

2 If fRog JuMqS bY

3 WHy HaS dottY set hER tam HERE?

4 eerIE SPUttER On NeW bUS In CiTY

5 OLD liONS arE telLINg Gnu jOKES

6 soTed iNvITED cisSY DRum

MUSICAL FLAGS

Instead of hunting for broken letters, code crackers can search for flags on musical notes:

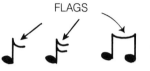

FLAGS

As you glide from left to right, pick out the letters that appear directly below the notes with flags:

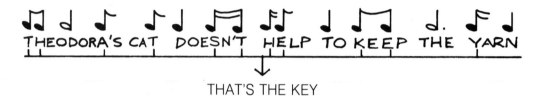

THEODORA'S CAT DOESN'T HELP TO KEEP THE YARN

THAT'S THE KEY

TRY THE KEY: CRACK THE CODES

1 APRIL RAINS UPON THE GRASSY LANES

2 SHE NODS WHEN OUR DAY ENDS

3 SO QUIET ARE THE LILIES AND REEDS

4 WHERE O WHERE ARE SHEBA AND ZACK?

5 AFTER A RAINY – WET DAY,

ARE THE FIREFLIES AT BAY?

Remember your pledge not to mark the pages. Keep every code an ironclad never-tell.

6

BLACK-EYED SUSANS

When you design this flowery notepaper, first bury a warning, a secret, or perhaps a password:

DUCK
UNDER

Then plant misleads to form sentences and border the sentences with petal-signaling "Susans."

The number of petals on a black-eyed Susan at the beginning of a sentence should tell a pal how many words to count **forward** to find the message word.

SHE HAS A DUCK AND TWO GEESE.

THEY'RE UNDER THE BRIDGE.

The number of petals on a "Susan" at the end of a sentence should signal how many words to count **backward** to uproot more of the message:

TRY THE KEY: CRACK THE CODES

1

PLEASE TAPE THE TORN CARD.
PLAY WITH THIS BRAND NEW DECK.

2

what will you wear?
I have your radio.
Head on over.
If kim phones, please tell me.

3

IT'S MY TURN.
BUT HANG AROUND.
SIT ON THE PORCH GLIDER.
It NEEDS A SEAT.
CAN YOU REPAIR IT?

7

VIDEO ZAP

Scan each screen from left to right, top to bottom. Look for the colored zingers: ● When you spot one, note the letter that follows. The letter may be in upper or lower case, but it doesn't matter. Mixing the cases is a codemaker's trick to quash the curious. Just hitch together the coded letters and **ZAP** out everything but the hidden message.

TRY THE KEY: CRACK THE CODES

PRINTOUTS

The key to this computer code is the word **PRINT**. When you see **PRINT**, look at the word or word group above it. Strung together—from top to bottom—the coded words will reveal the secret data stored in the machine's memory.

TRY THE KEY: CRACK THE CODES

To find the answer to each riddle, "run" the appropriate program.

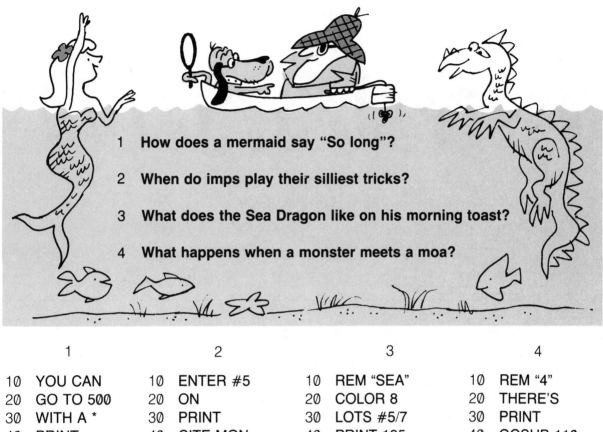

1 How does a mermaid say "So long"?

2 When do imps play their silliest tricks?

3 What does the Sea Dragon like on his morning toast?

4 What happens when a monster meets a moa?

	1		2		3		4
10	YOU CAN	10	ENTER #5	10	REM "SEA"	10	REM "4"
20	GO TO 500	20	ON	20	COLOR 8	20	THERE'S
30	WITH A *	30	PRINT	30	LOTS #5/7	30	PRINT
40	PRINT	40	CITE MON.	40	PRINT 195	40	GOSUB 110
50	INPUT = P#	50	APRIL	50	OF "—"	50	NO
60	SEE DIAL	60	PRINT "K"	60	PRINT ** +	60	PRINT ##*
70	WAVE	70	MAY & JUNE	70	GOSUB 1600	70	YES
80	PRINT #-6	80	GO TO 130	80	RECALL 10	80	PERHAPS LESS
90	OR TWO	90	GHOUL'S	90	JELLY	90	GO TO "ASIA"
100	PRINT *7 >8	100	PRINT–THEN X	100	PRINT	100	MOA
110	INT: RETURN	110	BAT WINGS	110	START "WHALE"	110	PRINT *4
		120	"24 HOURS"	120	FISH	120	RIGHT SIDE
		130	DAY	130	PRINT *#**	130	LEFT
		140	PRINT	140	"HOOK/LINE"	140	PRINT
				150	"SINKER"	150	RUN

9

If a candy cane has four or more stripes, note the letter below it. It is part of a "sugar-coded" message. To discover the hidden word, lick away the misleads and see what's left.

TRY THE KEY: CRACK THE CODE

U P H E P P I P E R A M M I K N T

MATH-X-AMPLES

Sometimes, codes are based on the positions of the letters in the alphabet.

POSITION:	1	2	3	4	5	6	7	8	9	10	11	12	13	14	15	16	17	18	19	20	21	22	23	24	25	26
LETTER:	A	B	C	D	E	F	G	H	I	J	K	L	M	N	O	P	Q	R	S	T	U	V	W	X	Y	Z

TRY THE KEY: CRACK THE CODES

Figure out the correct answer for each "math problem." Then match the number of the answer with the letter of the alphabet to uncover the word-X-change between Beth and Ellen.

Beth:
$$\begin{array}{ccccccc} & 10 & & & & & \\ 10 & 10 & 4 & 9 & 9 & 8 \\ +\ 3 & -2 & +1 & \times 2 & -4 & +4 \end{array}$$

$$\begin{array}{ccc} & 7 & & \\ 25 & 4 & 5 \\ -\ 5 & \times 2 & \times 1 \end{array}$$

$$\begin{array}{ccccc} & & & & 15 \\ 13 & 7 & 9 & 18 & 5 \\ +3 & -6 & +9 & \div 2 & +5 \end{array}$$

Ellen:
$$\begin{array}{cc} 6 & 5 \\ -5 & \times 4 \end{array}$$

$$\begin{array}{cccccc} & & & 9 & & \\ 5 & 3 & 14 & 8 & 11 & 12 & 2 & 16 \\ -3 & \times 7 & +12 & +9 & -10 & +6 & \times 2 & +3 \end{array}$$

$$\begin{array}{ccccc} 15 & 4 & 3 & 10 & 6 \\ -13 & \times 3 & \times 7 & -4 & \times 1 \end{array}$$

Beth:
$$\begin{array}{ccc} 7 & & \\ 5 & 1 & 19 \\ +1 & -0 & +6 \end{array}$$

$$\begin{array}{c} 3 \\ \times 3 \end{array}$$

$$\begin{array}{cccc} & & 5 & \\ 13 & 3 & 6 & 12 \\ -10 & \times 5 & +2 & -7 \end{array}$$

Ellen:
$$\begin{array}{cccc} 16 & 11 & 6 & 8 \\ +3 & +10 & \times 3 & -3 \end{array}$$

$$\begin{array}{cccc} 5 & 9 & 7 & 10 \\ +8 & -4 & -2 & +10 \end{array}$$

$$\begin{array}{cc} 9 & 11 \\ +4 & -6 \end{array}$$

$$\begin{array}{cccc} & & 14 & \\ 4 & 3 & 2 & 6 \\ \times 2 & +2 & +2 & -1 \end{array}$$

HIDING AMONG THE DIAMONDS

You can send messages to your friends through a deck of cards spread casually on a table. Each card could have a numerical value, like this:

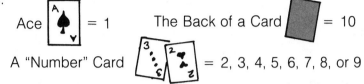

Ace = 1   The Back of a Card = 10

A "Number" Card = 2, 3, 4, 5, 6, 7, 8, or 9

By looking at a numeral or adding up the sum shown by a cluster of cards, a reader can figure out which letter of the alphabet comes into play. Use the Position Key on page 10.

10   10 + 5 = 15   1 + 10 = 11   5   10 + 8 = 18

J   O   K   E   R

TRY THE KEY: CRACK THE CODES

1

2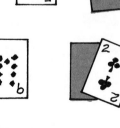

3

SKYSCRAPERS

Codes can also use position keys based on **reversed** alphabetical order. You can build messages into skyscrapers by reversing letters—from Z to A—according to these positions:

POSITION:	1	2	3	4	5	6	7	8	9	10	11	12	13	14	15	16	17	18	19	20	21	22	23	24	25	26
LETTER:	Z	Y	X	W	V	U	T	S	R	Q	P	O	N	M	L	K	J	I	H	G	F	E	D	C	B	A

Each row of windows will show the position of a letter. Use these designs and the values they stand for:

$$| = | \qquad \blacksquare = 5 \qquad \blacksquare = 10$$

When pals view your skylines, they can uncover the secret word in each building by taking these three steps:

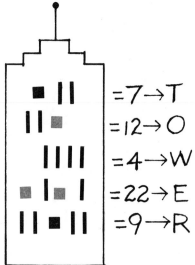

Step 1   Adding up the value of the windows **across** each row.

Step 2   Matching the sum in each row with the appropriate letter in the Reverse Position Key above.

Step 3   Reading the word made from the letters written top to bottom.

TRY THE KEY: CRACK THE CODES

13

IRAQI-WACKI

"It must be Arabic!" That's what you hope snoopers will think if they stumble across a message in Iraqi-Wacki.

The hidden word or words can be written in script from the top of the page to the bottom. Or they can run at an angle or upside down.

 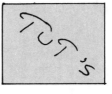 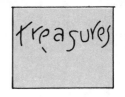

But the message is entombed by misleads that look like the markings in an ancient language. A code cracker simply turns an Iraqi-Wacki until its message pops off the page:

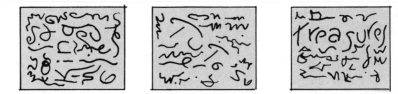

TRY THE KEY: CRACK THE CODES

Find the password in each box:

1   2   3

From left to right, what message does each row of boxes bury?

4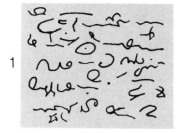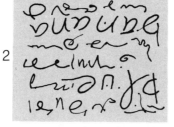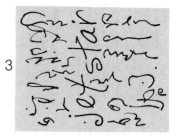

5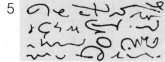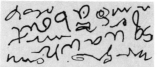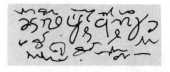

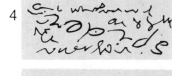 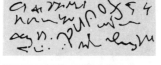 

TWIN-KLERS

For starry-eyed spies, break up a secret message so it reads correctly from left to right, top to bottom. METEOR =

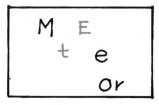

Put a star before and after each part.

Sprinkle misleads of other letters and stars. But beware! Do not place any misleading letters **between** twin-klers. Otherwise, even stargazers will think you're off your orbit.

TRY THE KEY: CRACK THE CODES

HINT: Hidden letters should be read only on the line in which they are star-coded. In other words, a star at the end of a line does **not** signal the first letter on the next line.

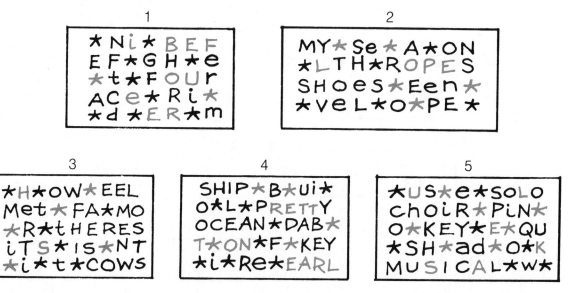

HUE CLUES

To understand how Hue Clues work, zoom in on every letter in a colored box. Then, for each, write down the letter that **follows** in the alphabet.

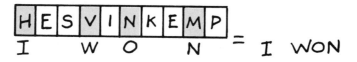

$$\begin{array}{ccccccccc} H & E & S & V & I & N & K & E & M & P \end{array}$$
$$\quad I \quad\quad W \quad\quad O \quad\quad N \quad = \; I \; WON$$

To write in this code, follow these steps:

Step 1   Print your secret message lightly in pencil. Vary the spacing between the letters.

Step 2   Think of the letter that comes immediately **before** each letter in the message, and write it firmly. Box each letter and color it in: any hue will do. To signal the letter **A** in a message, put Z in a box and dab it with color, too.

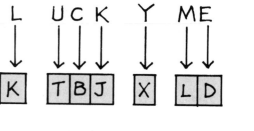

Step 3   Erase the penciled message and hitch up some uncolored sidetrackers in the empty spaces.

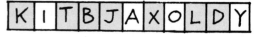

TRY THE KEY: CRACK THE CODES

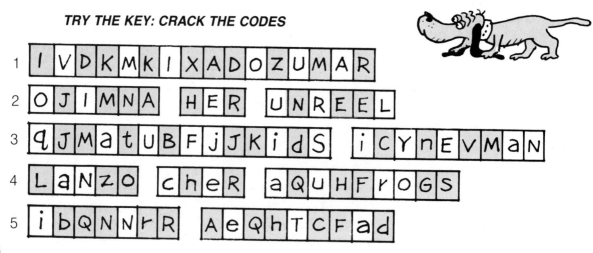

1   I V D K M K I X A D O Z U M A R

2   O J I M N A   H E R   U N R E E L

3   q J M a t u B F j j K i d S   i C Y n E V M a N

4   L a N Z o   c h e R   a Q u H F r o G S

5   i b Q N N r R   A e Q h T C F a d

16

PATCHES OF COLOR

Instead of boxing the "backup letters," as in Hue Clues, weave them into patches you design. Then let any colored letter in a patch or all the letters in a colored patch hide your message—blurred, of course, by miscues.

TRY THE KEY: CRACK THE CODES

1   What did the queen think of her stupid husband?

2   What does WZZZ call its midnight headlines?

3   What did the quick-tempered doctor lose?

TURTLES

See which way the turtle is heading (⟵ or ⟶), and **read in the same direction.** Read only the letters right below the lines that go up and down the turtle's shell. Ignore the dodo stumpers in the spaces between the lines.

TRY THE KEY: CRACK THE CODE

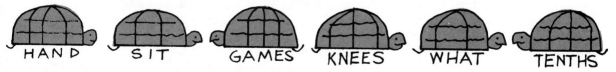

CODE BOWS

Look only at the bows in this position: . They contain letters in the coded message. Can you untie it?

TRY THE KEY: CRACK THE CODE

PHONY BALONEY

You and secret clubmates can use each other's telephone numbers to hide messages of up to seven words. For example, Mark's phone number is: **202-7493**

So when Mark's friend Tom penned the warning shown at the right, here's what he did. He placed the first coded word (**ISLAND**) next to the numeral 2, the first digit in Mark's phone number. The second word (**FERRY**) he hid next to the 10, which stands for the 0 in Mark's phone number.

1. THE
2. ISLAND, LEAVES
3. —
4. AT, ONCE
5. TUESDAY
6. WINDY
7. HARBOR
8. RED, LIGHTHOUSE
9. MIDNIGHT
10. FERRY

Tom also wrote the third coded word (**LEAVES**) next to the 2, as shown. He then completed the message by placing coded words after the 7, the 4, and the 9. But because his message ran only six rather than seven words, Tom scratched a dash next to the 3, which is the seventh and last digit in Mark's phone number. The dash means "there are no more words in this message."

Finally, Tom added misleads to steer snoops afar. What warning was he shielding from them?

TRY THE KEY: CRACK THE CODES

1	Tim's Number 321-7615	2	Arlene's Number 583-7624	3	Rita's Number 953-4162
1	YOU, TELL	1	HE, the	1	More
2	CAN	2	Pen	2	GUM
3	WHEN	3	BORROW	3	Have, STICKY
4	HIM	4	—	4	ANY
5	ME	5	MAY, JUNE	5	YOU
6	FISHING	6	Ballpoint	6	BUBBLE
7	GO	7	Your	7	Trouble
8	SAILING	8	I	8	CANDY, MAKE
9	AT NOON	9	RULER	9	DO
10	TOMORROW	10	Money, PIGS	10	Boiling

4	Mario's Number 454-9183	5	Sum Yee's Number 632-1901	6	Harold's Number 627-5273
1	MY	1	YESTERDAY, GAME	1	DaNNy
2	Green, Bumpy	2	IT	2	GAVe, PIECE
3	LAWN	3	LOST	3	BILL
4	After, HAVE	4	SCORE, A	4	Me
5	I	5	HIGH, PITCHED	5	LAST
6	Met, With	6	I	6	I
7	OUR	7	WON	7	MY, TO
8	NEIGHBOR'S	8	STRIKES, THREE	8	CoST
9	Mowed	9	DURING	9	OncE, seND
10	DOWN	10	THE	10	PoSTcArD

19

LOOP THE LETTERS

Turn to lined paper to loop a code. Start at the upper right-hand corner and "loop" the letters in your message from top to bottom to top to bottom, as shown by the numerals in the boxed example. There, the word **S-H-A-R-E** loops like this:

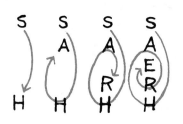

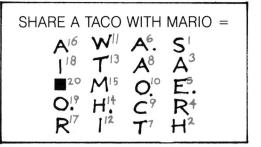

SHARE A TACO WITH MARIO =

A[16] W[11] A.[6] S[1]
I[18] T[13] A[8] A[3]
■[20] M[15] O.[10] E.[5]
O.[19] H.[14] C[9] R[4]
R[17] I[12] T[7] H[2]

Always begin a column of letters at the top. When a word ends, put a period after the last letter. Mark the end of a sentence with a dark square.

TRY THE KEY: CRACK THE CODE

HINT: As you unravel this message, be sure to count each dark square as if it were just another letter in the looping pattern. The first word is **BEWARE**. What is the rest of the writer's warning?

E.	O	r	e	N	G	c	t	M	B
E	T	v	a	p	t.	A.	N	y.	w
e	E	R.	f	A	N.	L	G	R	r
O	e.	S	r	K.	o	S	T.	E	■
f.	T	E.	i	m	r.	L	P	i	o
■	h	Y	n.	e	K	i	A	N.	G.
L	■	e	K.	■	U	H	■	P.	F
w	R	■	O	C	Y	a	H	E	e.
r	H	E	t.	s	i	f	i	C	a
w	U.	i	T.	a	H	K.	O	a	E

20

A RIDDLE-BRICK WALL

When a bungling bozo smacks up against something like this, it does indeed feel like a brick wall.

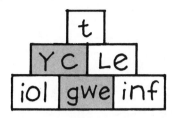

But a spy who holds the key can easily pass through. In this case, each coded letter has a line above it:  . Other letters and the colored blocks are bozo-boffos. When the coded letters are read left to right, beginning at the top, the secret message tumbles forth:

CLOWN

TRY THE KEY: CRACK THE CODES

1 What makes clouds comfy to sleep on?

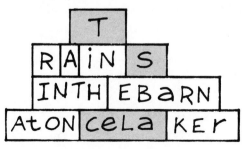

2 In the race to grow fastest, what couldn't Tiny Tomato do?

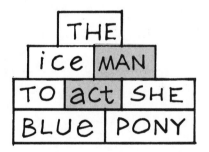

3 What's the opposite of an uncle muncher?

4 What did people call the fat knight?

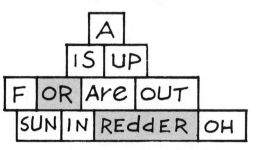

CLASSIFIED

WANTED: PALS WITH THE KEY TO THIS CODE

Here's how it works. Look at the telephone number in the want ad. The area code shown in parentheses (723) signals the positions of three coded letters—when they are counted from the left to the right in the first line (P-I-R). The next three numerals (245) reveal which letters are hidden in the second line (A-T-E). And the third set of numerals (8127) tells which secret letters are tucked into the third line (S-H-I-P).

Only the first three lines in a want ad contain a hidden message, as in P-I-R-A-T-E S-H-I-P. A fourth line is always a mislead that steers sneak peekers far afield.

HINT: When you come to a zero (0) in a telephone number, it signals the end of a coded message.

TRY THE KEY: CRACK THE CODES

1

RIBS + CHOPS
BEN'S GROCERY
NO. DARBY

(312) 358-4137

2

DEEJAYS
Save On Records
SALE
"PLATTER MATTERS"
(451) 832-1400

3

Green House Special
EASTER ORCHIDS
R.B. Webster, Florist
(681) 597-5382

4

GIANT BARGAINS
KARP'S MART
DELANEY AVENUE
(629) 473-8160

22

TYPING GRIDS

The main keys on a typewriter and a host of computers form this kind of grid:

With a similar layout, you can send codes using only dots and numerals. The numerals stand for columns, and the dots represent letters in a column.

For example, **MOHAWK** would be coded this way:

with **M** found three spaces below the **7**; **O** one space below the **9**; and so on. Color some of the dots to throw code pokers "off key."

TRY THE KEY: CRACK THE CODES

Which state name comes from the Indian word that has the meaning shown above the grid?

1 Land of Tomorrow

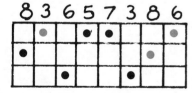

2 Long River Place

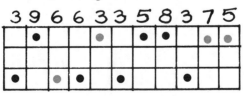

3 South Wind People

4 Great Water

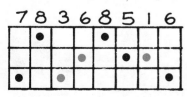

5 One Who Puts to Sleep

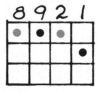

6 Large Prairie Place

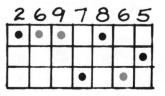

MILE MARKERS

When you come to an intersection on Code Road, here's how to read the mile markers.

See which way an arrow points. It tells you from which side to start counting the letters in the name of the town:

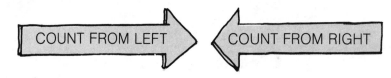

COUNT FROM LEFT   COUNT FROM RIGHT

The numerals tell you how far to count. When the numeral is a single digit, you count that many letters left or right:

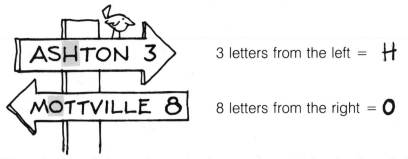

ASHTON 3   3 letters from the left = H

MOTTVILLE 8   8 letters from the right = O

With a double digit, seek out the letters signaled by the first digit, then those signaled by the second. Record the message so it follows the order of all the digits from top to bottom. On this page, for example, the four markers on this post ask: **HOW FAR?**

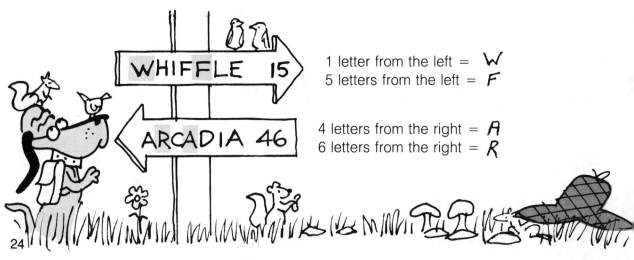

WHIFFLE 15   1 letter from the left = W
5 letters from the left = F

ARCADIA 46   4 letters from the right = A
6 letters from the right = R

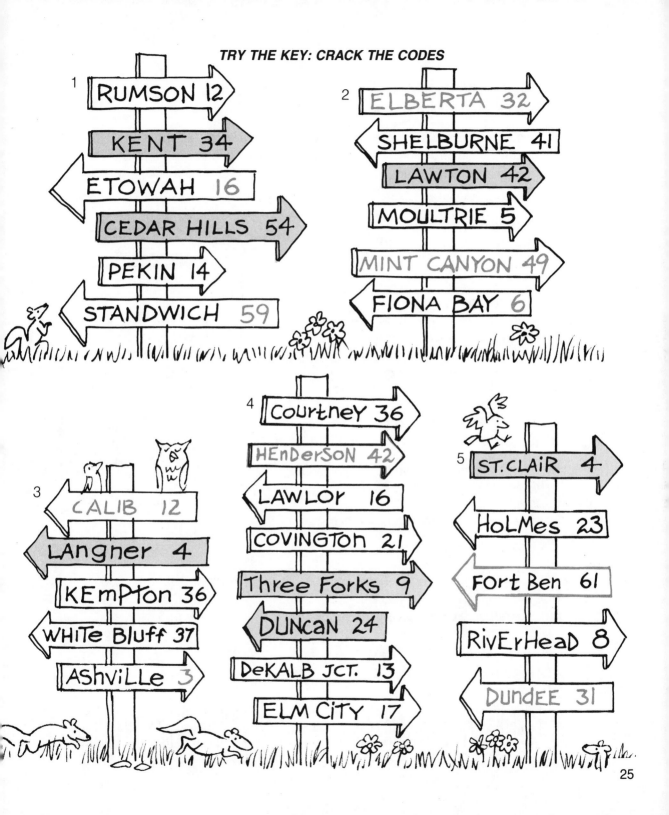

TRY THE KEY: CRACK THE CODES

1. RUMSON 12
   KENT 34
   ETOWAH 16
   CEDAR HILLS 54
   PEKIN 14
   STANDWICH 59

2. ELBERTA 32
   SHELBURNE 41
   LAWTON 42
   MOULTRIE 5
   MINT CANYON 49
   FIONA BAY 6

3. CALIB 12
   LANGNER 4
   KEMPTON 36
   WHITE BLUFF 37
   ASHVILLE 3

4. COURTNEY 36
   HENDERSON 42
   LAWLOR 16
   COVINGTON 21
   THREE FORKS 9
   DUNCAN 24
   DEKALB JCT. 13
   ELM CITY 17

5. ST. CLAIR 4
   HOLMES 23
   FORT BEN 61
   RIVERHEAD 8
   DUNDEE 31

STUFF 'N BLUFF

There's more to this code than a couple of calories. Markings on each product tell you how to uncover a hidden message.

A numeral signals how far **down** to count in the list of words that describe the product. The line or lines above a numeral tell how many letters **within** the word to count.

How far down to count **5** = 5

How far in to count ||||| = 4

In the example at the right, the first letter is keyed like this: |||
4 . That means the first letter of the message can be found in the **fourth** word (SUGAR), and it is the **third** letter (|||) in the word: G.

The second letter in the message can be found in the **third** word down the list (SODIUM), and it is the **second** (||) letter: O.

So the first word in the message is GO. What's the rest?

CALORIES	140
FAT	3g
SODIUM	155mg
SUGAR	1g

4 3 2 1   4   3   2

TRY THE KEY: CRACK THE CODES

1

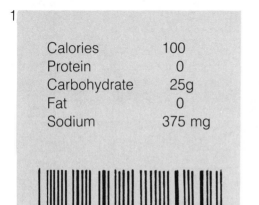

Calories	100
Protein	0
Carbohydrate	25g
Fat	0
Sodium	375 mg

1 3 2 3 1   3 5 2 5 3

2

Portions	6
Calories	120
Carbohydrate	9g
Fat	2g
Sodium	35mg

2 5 2 3 1 5 4 1 2 5

DOTTED COLUMNS

Break up your message in rows of letters. Add misleads, if necessary, to complete the bottom row.

Then look at the **columns** of letters as if they were numbered . . .

but code these columns for a friend by scrambling their order and inserting dots **or** numerals among the letters to signal which column is referred to. As the examples below show, you don't have to place the dots together, but you can arrange them any way on a line. Beware: do not scramble the letters **within** the columns.

WAIT FOR ANN

WAI
TFO
RAN
NKZ

Columns
↓ ↓ ↓
1 2 3
WAI
TFO
RAN
NKZ

Your friend needs only to reconstruct the order of the columns—**without the dots and numerals**—to read the letters in the message from left to right, top to bottom.

•AFAK• → These letters form the 2ᵈ column.
WT•RN → These letters form the 1ˢᵗ column.
IONZ3 ↘ These letters form the 3ᵈ column.

TRY THE KEY: CRACK THE CODES

1

E5NJ
•UEA••
4RAD
•YAH
•OBE•

2

••ESDE•
1THEL
CL5MK
6EREM
••IAYD••
•HAAT•

3

CNITR3
U••UBCA
TTRIN•
5IEDOX
••KDGIY••

4

F••SAY•••
HRNO•
O1GMZ
U•MGN•
NID•••D
TSI4X

OOPS MEMO: Keep these pages free of trail markers. Use separate pieces of paper to figure out the puzzlers.

EINSTEIN'S STUMPER

What's all that mumbo jumbo below? Is it a formula by Einstein?

No, it's an entry in Wendy's diary. Her coded letters—in upper and lower case—are framed by **parentheses** $(LIKE)(th)(I_2S)$ Other letters and markings are misleads, including the numerals that also appear in the parentheses.

TRY THE KEY: CRACK THE CODE

Reading left to right, what did Wendy wish?

$$(DE) \times M_4\, Cl = (AR)\,(DI_3\, A) \div 30 \times 7 = (R_3\, Y)$$

$$4(z) = (I\, P_2)\ BH_2N\ (TI)\, 5 - \left\langle \frac{(GHT^3)}{[4-5]} \right\rangle - (M) \div (YSE) \times 46\ (CRE) = (TS)$$

$$\left\langle {}^{Hn}_{\ Hn} \right\rangle = (S_5 O) \times 4.51 = (AK) - \underset{F\ell}{\overset{F\ell}{\langle\rangle}} - X_2\ (M^3 YT) = (e) - 3\ (AR_s)$$

$$\frac{4}{PR} \times 3^* = (WR) + (Apm) < \underset{Kt}{\overset{Kt}{\langle\ \rangle}} = (Y) \div 3B + (SM^2)\,(I) = 4J\ (LE^s)$$

$$(I) + 4(n) = \begin{smallmatrix} & 5 & \\ 5 & & 5 \\ 5 & & 5 \\ & 5 & \end{smallmatrix} \times (K) = Cl_2 N > (AL_3) \div (Lm) + (V) = \underset{4}{\overset{4}{\langle\ \rangle}} \times (D) + 4\ (AY$$

$$CN_2 + (F_0) - D = (Re) > 5\,(v) = (Er)$$

MOTH CODES AND BUTTERFLIES

When telegraph machines started clickety-clacking in the late 1800s, they were sending messages in code by electrical wire. Named for its inventor, Samuel F. B. Morse, the code consists of dots (quick taps of the telegraph key), dashes (slightly longer taps), and pauses:

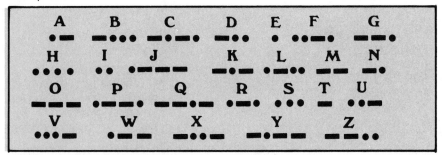

Today you can use the Morse code to hide messages in butterfly markings. Simply "telegraph" your letters from left to right across **both** wings and from top to bottom. Draw puddly circles and tiny freckles around the dots and dashes to camouflage your piece of

TRY THE KEY: CRACK THE CODES

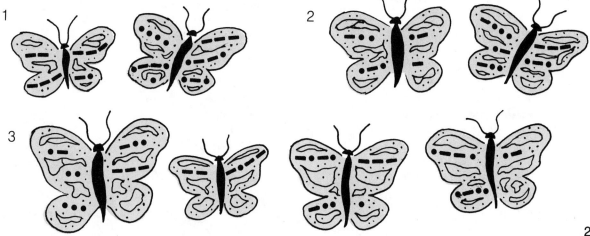

ANSWER FILE

BREAKER MAKERS, page 4
1   PHONE ME
2   ROUND UP
3   BURIED SKULL
4   JILL LOVES AL
5   IN MOSS SWAMP

BEGINNER'S SCRAWL, page 5
1   CLIMB UP
2   BUG OFF
3   MATH TEST TODAY
4   IN BENT TREE
5   JUNGLE TRAIL
6   MUSIC VIDEOS

MUSICAL FLAGS, page 6
1   RING ALAN
2   SEND WORD
3   SQUEALER
4   HORSEBACK
5   FARAWAY REEF

BLACK-EYED SUSANS, page 7
1   TAPE DECK
2   WEAR YOUR HEADPHONES
3   MY HANG GLIDER NEEDS REPAIR

VIDEO ZAP, page 8
1   SPACE INVADERS
2   WHAT'S THE ANSWER?
3   FIND GREEN CLIP
4   ARE YOU SCARED, TOO?

PRINTOUTS, pages 8–9
1   WITH A WAVE OR TWO
2   ON APRIL GHOUL'S DAY
3   LOTS OF JELLYFISH
4   THERE'S NO MOA LEFT

CANDY CANES, page 10
PEPPERMINT

MATH-X-AMPLES, page 10
BETH: WHERE'S THE PARTY?
ELLEN: AT BUZZARD'S BLUFF.
BETH: MAY I COME?
ELLEN: SURE. MEET ME HERE.

HIDING AMONG THE DIAMONDS, page 11
1   FIG BAR
2   WE LEFT
3   SILVER COIN

SKYSCRAPERS, pages 12–13
1   HERE'S TO A FRIEND
2   HOPE YOU ARE OKAY
3   BEST WISHES FROM CUZZY

IRAQI-WACKI, page 14
1   UNICORN
2   BLUE BANANA
3   JETSTAR
4   SPIDER FOUND CLUBHOUSE
5   DON'T SQUAWK ABOUT YOUR GRADES

TWIN-KLERS, page 15
1   NIGHTRIDER
2   SEAL THE ENVELOPE
3   HOW FAR IS IT?
4   BUILD A BONFIRE
5   USE PINK EYE SHADOW

HUE CLUES, page 16
1   JELLYBEANS
2   KNOB IS OFF
3   KNUCKLE DOWN
4   MAP IS RIGHT
5   CROSS BRIDGE

Mr. Albert is also the author of CODES FOR KIDS and MORE CODES FOR KIDS. "To create a code," says Burton Albert, "I noodle and doodle. That's what I call fiddling with words and making sketches on my yellow legal pad." For CODE BUSTERS! however, his first idea popped into mind while he was delayed in an airport for five hours—without a pad to write on! He had to scribble the notes for these codes in the white spaces of ads in a newspaper.

Artist Jerry Warshaw has illustrated numerous riddle books, including CHICKEN RIDDLE, MERRY-GO-RIDDLE, and THE RIDDLE AGES. He is also the author of THE FUNNY DRAWING BOOK and THE I CAN'T DRAW BOOK. Mr. Warshaw lives in Evanston, Illinois, with his wife and daughter, an orange and white cat named Friskin, a newt, a guinea pig, and two gerbils.